OUR RESCUE DOG
Family Album

Written by
DIANE POMERANCE, Ph.D.

POLAIRE
PUBLICATIONS
Flower Mound, Texas

Printed in the United States of America
First Printing: February 2010

14 13 12 11   010   1 2 3 4 5

Cover and text design by Diane Pomerance, Ph.D.
and Crystal Wood, Tattersall Publishing, Denton, Texas
Author Family and Extended Family portraits by Don Barnes/The Photographers

Photos contributed by Don and Dee Barnes, Betty Christenson,
Sherrie and John Narusis, and Drs. Diane and Norman Pomerance.

For more information, write to:
Polaire Publications
PMB 217
2221 Old Justin Road, Ste. 119
Flower Mound, Texas 75028

www.animalcompanionsandtheirpeople.com

ISBN: 978-0-9795218-8-1

Library of Congress Control Number: 2009909462

Dedication

To the countless beautiful, innocent and vulnerable animals in need of our love, respect and appreciation – in need of food and shelter – in need of safe and loving homes – and to those kind, caring, and compassionate human beings who have, and continue to, come to their aid.

The author and one of her rescue dogs, Tobias.

"Our task must be to free ourselves by widening our circle of compassion to embrace all living creatures and the whole of nature and its beauty."
— Albert Einstein

"By ethical conduct toward all creatures we enter a spiritual relationship with the universe."

— Albert Schweitzer

Introduction

Each year millions of innocent animals are neglected, abandoned, abused, disregarded and discarded. They suffer needlessly, senselessly and mercilessly and are tortured and tormented by heartless individuals who have little respect for themselves let alone any other living creature.

The more "fortunate" strays and castoffs are surrendered to animal shelters, welfare organizations or rescue organizations where (if they are extremely lucky) they will get adopted by a caring and compassionate person or family. The less fortunate animals live on dangerous city streets darting in and out of traffic, barely surviving, sick, starving and injured—drinking foul or contaminated water and eating garbage out of gutters and dumpsters. Some of the less fortunate animals live feral lives in city suburbs, woods or rural areas exposed constantly to all the elements without food or water. Theirs is a constant battle to survive.

Our beautiful Cassie before rescue

Others are kept tethered to a backyard tree or confined to a tiny fenced-in area and are left to die of thirst and/or starvation. They are left outside in the frigid cold, torrential rain, fierce wind, or intense and relentless heat. Others find their way to abandoned or uninhabited homes, apartments, lean-tos or other temporary shelters. Many endure the harshest, most abhorrent, inhumane and heartbreaking circumstances. Others are captured by animal control and will be placed in a municipal animal shelter for a short time while experiencing terrible stress, trauma, terror, fear and duress until they are either adopted or euthanized.

Countless innocent, helpless and defenseless animals suffer unnecessarily at the hands of humans. They endure the horrors of torture, violence, abuse and mutilation. Many are the victims of greedy and irresponsible "backyard" breeders or puppy mill owners and are bred constantly until they are no longer capable of breeding due to old age or ill health. Their puppies are sold roadside, through the Internet, as well as newspaper and magazine ads.

They are purchased by pet store owners or individuals looking for "purebred" dogs, cats or other animals. In many cases, the breeding dogs exist in indescribably deplorable and inhumane conditions and are often kept in small wire "cages" in which they are physically unable to comfortably stand, let alone move around, throughout their entire lives. Their cages and the cages of their puppies and other breeding dogs are often piled upon each other. The dogs are inadequately fed and provided with insufficient or filthy water and little (if any) veterinary care. They often live soaked in their own urine and covered with their own feces. Many are sick with heartworm, intestinal worms and other serious medical problems. Many live in constant pain and receive no medical attention. Others have broken bones or jaws; some are without teeth, paws, tails, ears or fur. It is almost unfathomable to imagine the misery and horror of the lives of these sentient, loving creatures.

Were it not for human ignorance, carelessness, thoughtlessness, self-preoccupation, selfishness and a lack of compassion, these vulnerable and defenseless animals might be living comfortably, safely and contentedly by our sides as our happy, healthy, devoted and unconditionally loving "best friends" and family members. They might be living joyously and harmoniously, sharing their love and affection with us, while also serving as our friends, teachers, guides and healers. The benefits of animal companionship are scientifically well substantiated and include increased longevity and quality of life, as well as improved physical, psychological, and emotional health. The simple act of petting an animal friend has proven to be of significant physical and psychological benefit. His presence has a calming effect. Blood pressure is reduced. Heartbeat is improved. Our animal companions reduce our stress, fear and anger; they also decrease loneliness, anxiety and depression.

It is my sincerest hope and wish that the readers of this book are inspired to rescue or adopt an animal in need. The rewards of adopting such an animal are immeasurable. The joy of living with and caring for them as they recover, blossom and flourish is boundless.

~ Diane Pomerance, Ph.D.

...and friends...

Our Rescue Dog Family Album

The rescue dogs who appear in this book are as follows.
They have all been adopted by and have been or are currently
dearly loved members of the Pomerance family.

Jasper
Yorkshire Terrier

Reggie
Yorkshire Terrier

Agatha Beasley
Maltese mix

Katie I
German Shepherd

Kaitlyn
German Shepherd

Caesar
Alaskan Malamute/
Lab mix

Spencer
German Shepherd/
Rottweiler mix

Sophie
Dachshund/
Catahoula mix

Chloe
Beagle/
Foxhound mix

Tasha
Golden Retriever/
Chow mix

Kianna
Alaskan Malamute/
wolf mix

Dony
Alaskan Malamute/
Siberian Husky mix

Jasmine
Labrador Retriever

Bentley
German Shepherd

Kobuck
Alaskan Malamute

Bojangles
Siberian Husky mix

Emily
German Shepherd

Shadow
Siberian Husky

Cinders
Siberian Husky

Lumberjack
Alaskan Malamute

Nenani
Alaskan Malamute

Tobias
Alaskan Malamute

Hitchcock
Siberian
Husky mix

Sunny
Labrador
Retriever

Innoko
Alaskan Malamute/
Siberian Husky mix

Maximus
Anatolian
Shepherd

Khanti
Alaskan Malamute

Diva
Alaskan Malamute

Angel
Alaskan Malamute

Tallon
Alaskan Malamute

oco Chanel
Dachshund

Two Socks
Alaskan Malamute

Shania
Alaskan Malamute

Kali
Alaskan Malamute

Cassie
Klee Kai

Mara
askan Malamute/
nan Shepherd mix

Higgins
Alaskan Malamute/
Labrador Retriever mix

Clarissa
Anatolian
Shepherd

Phoebe
Dachshund

Luddy
Dachshund

ucado
an Malamute/
an Shepherd mix

Fritz Henry
Dachshund/
MinPin mix

Eleanor
Dachshund/
MinPin mix

Each has a story
to share ...

I ♥ NY

Our first "rescue" dogs and I in NYC

JASPER

REGGIE

My husband, Norm, and I never set out to save or "rescue" animals. We simply loved them and have always had our own whom we regard as family members. Even when we were graduate students at the University of Michigan in Ann Arbor in the early 1970s and rented an apartment, which did not allow us to have a dog or cat, we had parakeets or turtles. We moved to New York City in 1976. As soon as we moved to an apartment in Manhattan that did permit us to have pets, we acquired our first "puppy mill" dogs from a pet store. Two Yorkshire terriers named **Jasper and Reggie** had been returned by their owners to the pet shop from which they had been purchased because of medical and size issues (Jasper was too large and overweight; Reggie was small and underweight.) Neither was a good example of the breed, and each had medical issues with which we had to contend. Both were skittish and frail, but we did our best to ensure that they received appropriate exercise, diet and veterinary care, along with a great deal of love and affection.

When we moved to Los Angeles in 1979, we made certain to find an apartment that allowed pets (a special fee or security deposit was required from us to cover any potential pet-related damage), and we, with Jasper and Reggie, happily lived together in a cul-de-sac in Hollywood where, it seemed everyone had dogs, cats, birds, or some other pet. While living in Hollywood, we were very surprised at the number of "stray" dogs we discovered that had been dumped by their owners. None of these dogs had identification tags, and virtually all of them were very friendly. I can't recall a single encounter with an aggressive or unfriendly dog. We were nonplussed by the seemingly never-ending number of animals that had been simply discarded and left on the streets in our neighborhood. Somehow, we managed to find homes for each of these animals, as we, legally, were not allowed to have more than three dogs.

As I was jogging one morning, I noticed a lovely little Maltese mix on the sidewalk near our apartment building wandering aimlessly as if lost. I went up to her and petted her gently. She was very friendly, and completely comfortable with me. She licked me all over my face as though I were her long-lost friend. She was utterly adorable and irresistible. Although she wore no collar or identification tag, I could not believe such a warm and gentle creature didn't belong to someone. After noticing that she was still roaming around our apartment building that evening and afraid that harm might come her way, we took her to our apartment. We attempted to find her owners, putting up signs around the building and area, spreading the word with friends and neighbors. However, after receiving no response whatsoever, we ended up keeping her.

She became our third dog – we named her **Agatha Beasley**. Amazingly, she got along beautifully with Jasper and Reggie from the moment they met, perhaps because she was a female and they were males. But this beautiful baby was meant to be a member of our family…and we grew to love and care for her deeply.

Several years after we moved to Los Angeles, in 1981, we purchased our first house in Sherman Oaks. It was situated high in the hills overlooking the San Fernando Valley. For the first time ever, we had our own fenced-in backyard, and our dogs could play and run to their heart's content. Once again, we lived in a cul-de-sac that served as a dumping ground for stray dogs and cats. Once again, my husband and I rose to the task (often very time-consuming and demanding) of finding good homes for them – and managed to save their lives.

When we moved to our next home in the San Fernando Valley (Tarzana) several years later, our first Yorkie, Jasper, died, and Agatha was

Agatha & Jasper get walkies!

Agatha, Jasper & "Grandpa Joe"

AGATHA

2

Agatha and Reggie
greet baby Katie

ill with leukemia. Little Reggie had somehow, inexplicably but discernibly, become old Reggie. He had periodontal disease, cataracts, walked slowly, had arthritis and was easily disoriented. While taking Reggie for a routine visit to our vet, a vet tech asked us if we would be interested in adopting a 6-week old German Shepherd who had been born to a backyard breeder and who had been hit by a car. She had a severely broken leg. I immediately said, "Yes" and fell in love with the beautiful little dog we adopted and subsequently named **Katie**. Katie's leg had required surgery, and she was wearing a large cast on her right hind leg, which she dragged clumsily but determinedly. She was truly beautiful and extremely alert and intelligent despite her young age and the pain I am certain she was experiencing.

We adopted Katie in mid-November. During a follow-up visit to our vet, we learned that her leg had not healed properly and that she would need to undergo further surgery. Her second surgery was scheduled a few days before Christmas. We were very worried, nervous and apprehensive about this young, small dog undergoing another surgery. We were shocked and horrified to receive a phone call from the animal hospital the afternoon following the surgery informing us that our tiny, delicate little girl never recovered from anesthesia. My husband and I were heartbroken – we deeply mourned the loss of this lovely, innocent creature that we had come to adore. We were beside ourselves with grief.

We literally cried in each other's arms for several days, and then decided to contact the vet and see if there had been other dogs in her litter that had survived. After learning that there were eight other dogs in her litter, we contacted the breeder and adopted Katie's sister – the female that most closely resembled her in appearance and spirit. We named her **Kaitlyn Cybill Shepherd (Katie II).** She was our Christmas gift in every sense of the word. She instantly got along well with Agatha and Reggie, and our new Katie was our pride and joy.

Our house in Tarzana, California

Kaitlyn Cybill Shepherd

KATIE II

Katie was our first "big" dog – she was the dog I'd always dreamed of having – clever, wise, beautiful, spirited, loyal – always by my side. We bonded immediately, and it felt as though we had known each other forever. She was so attuned to my husband and me – she was extremely intuitive and empathetic – seemingly able to "read our minds" and understand our thoughts. I would simply think of a command or plan, and she would understand and act upon it. We shared an extraordinary relationship!

Katie was so very intelligent, we felt obliged to "obedience" train her and took her to several doggie socialization classes and training programs. She performed beautifully. We then decided to have her trained by a professional trainer on a one-on-one basis. Her trainer was Miriam, a former member of the Israeli army – definitely a "no nonsense" type. She had been referred to us by a friend. There was no gushing over how beautiful Katie was or how intelligent she was from Miriam. Only Katie's performance, behavior and response to commands mattered to Miriam, and a particularly important part of Miriam's focus was to teach Katie to heel – to have Katie walk with us "correctly" and appropriately on a leash. Katie had a tendency to become distracted and to bark at other dogs when on a walk with us. We walked with her in our subdivision and she learned to "heel" fairly well and consistently. At a large nearby park, however, it was a different story. There were so many distractions – roller bladers, joggers, children running and bicycle riding, laughing and screaming, and jumping rope. Katie became a "wild" girl who either "hunkered down" and refused to budge or leaped forward, lunged, tugged, or

zigzagged in front of me all the while barking ferociously and furiously at other people and dogs who happened to be walking by. Miriam had repeatedly suggested that a canine companion about Katie's size would calm her down.

On one especially momentous afternoon during one of Katie's "walking in the park and heeling" lessons, we encountered a large stray dog who seemed to be accompanying us (from afar) as we attempted to teach Katie to heel. He was a creamy white and golden Alaskan Malamute/Labrador Retriever mix with hauntingly beautiful and gentle, large brown eyes, a beautiful deep grey mask, a widow's peak, and floppy ears. He had evidently been terribly abused – he was emaciated, had numerous scars over all of his body and was absolutely terrified of humans. He was, however, obviously smitten by our beautiful Katie as he followed Miriam, Norman and me around the park, generally keeping a safe distance away from us. Although Katie barked at him, her heart did not seem truly invested in chasing him away. She appeared flattered by his attention and impressed by his independence and ability to avoid being captured (rescued). It was as though he was literally "courting" our Kate. He came up to her and sniffed her from head to tail. His tail never stopped wagging. He postured, he posed, he strutted – he was clearly out to impress her. Although Norm, Miriam and I could not get close to him, he managed to come close enough to Kate to put his head on her shoulders and to gently lick her. We fell in love with this poor, pitiful stray dog. It was not long before word spread throughout the park about the stray that needed to be rescued. Soon we were joined by a number of people who were helping to pursue the dog in order to save him from an almost certain death. We had an extra leash and collar in our car—I ran to get it. We chased the dog, but he constantly eluded us. Finally, the heat of the day and sheer exhaustion overcame him.

Always smiling....

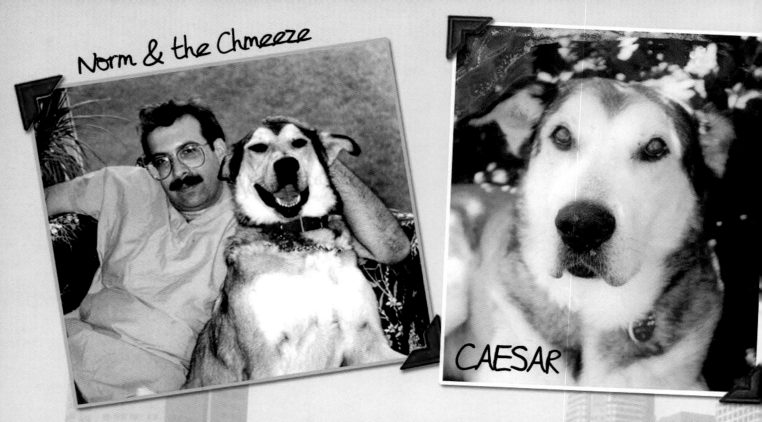

Norm & the Chmeeze

CAESAR

He was a very clever, resourceful boy, and he finally succumbed to our well-intentioned pursuit. I had already made the decision to adopt him, but I knew Norm hadn't arrived at the same conclusion. We asked our Iranian acquaintance who was responsible for finding this dog to name him – she named him **Caesar** in honor of a beautiful and beloved dog she had loved and lost as a child. We knew he bore no resemblance to the arrogant and able warrior "Caesar," but in her dog's honor and in accordance with her wishes, we so named him. He was never a "Caesar"; he was soft, plush and vulnerable and by no means royal or regal. We nicknamed him **"the Chmeeze"** and he remained "the Chmeeze" forever in our hearts and our minds.

Ultimately, with the help of many other animal-loving and compassionate people in the park, we finally managed to corner him and place the collar and leash on him. He was shaking terribly. We managed to get him in our car and immediately took him to our vet (whose office was near our house and the park), so that he could be examined and treated for his wounds and have his overall physical condition assessed. We were aware that we could not bring him home without having him checked for fleas, ticks or any other medical issues that might have jeopardized the health of our other dogs.

Caesar spent several days at the vet—he did not have any life-threatening injuries or health issues, and, as he slowly began to recover, we decided to adopt him. With the assistance of our trainer, Miriam, and the Iranian girl who had helped save him, Caesar and Katie and Reggie (our Agatha had suddenly died) were introduced and learned to get along together. It took us several years to bring Caesar to full health and well being. For a very long time, Caesar would sit in a corner of our den and shiver anytime a stranger would come to visit. He also had a series of grand mal seizures and suffered terrible separation anxiety whenever my husband and I would leave him home alone. We never felt comfortable boarding him or leaving him at home when we were gone, so we recruited a coterie of animal-loving and reliable house- and dog-sitters to care for him and the other dogs.

Caesar was always delicate and had many health problems, but the joy he brought us was indescribable and incalculable. He was wily, willful, playful, and an escape artist extraordinaire.

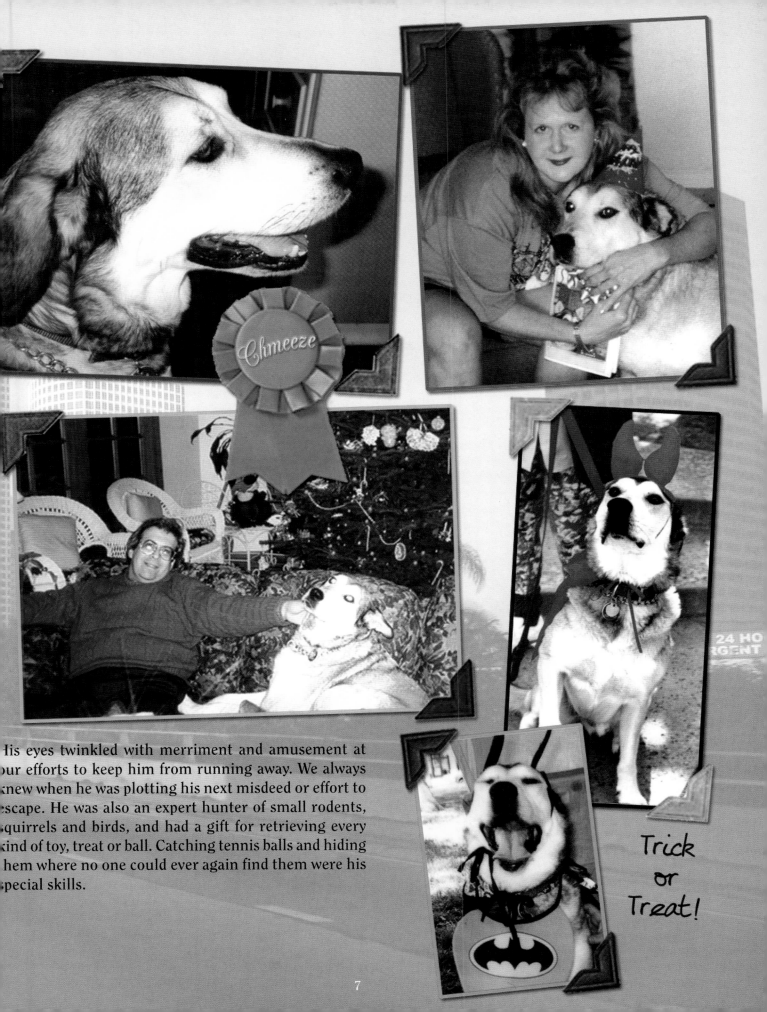

His eyes twinkled with merriment and amusement at our efforts to keep him from running away. We always knew when he was plotting his next misdeed or effort to escape. He was also an expert hunter of small rodents, squirrels and birds, and had a gift for retrieving every kind of toy, treat or ball. Catching tennis balls and hiding them where no one could ever again find them were his special skills.

Chmeeze

Trick or Treat!

SPENCER

Not too keen on baths...but a swim is different!

Spencer
& Chmeeze

Several years after we adopted Caesar, I was driving to my office, when I spotted a large Rottweiler/German Shepherd mix in an intersection in the San Fernando Valley. I pulled into the parking lot of a mini-mart and managed to persuade him to get out of traffic. He tried to eat some garbage out of one of the bins in the parking lot. I called to him. He was very friendly and got into my car immediately. I rewarded him with the dog biscuits I usually kept in my car. I asked anyone around if they knew where this dog belonged, who his owner was. No one had an idea, so I ended up taking this new, extremely loveable, good-natured and friendly huge dog to work with me. Everyone fell in love with the dog I named **Spencer**, but no one wanted to adopt him. I took him to my husband's office, hoping to entice someone there to adopt Spencer. No luck there either. I ended up bringing Spencer home with me. He and Caesar were not particularly fond of each other. They were tolerant but little more. Nonetheless, they were superb partners in crime. Spencer became a beloved member of the family for nearly 14 years, bringing great joy, laughter and fun to our lives. Spencer was a natural clown, a court jester and amazed us with the vast repertoire of "tricks" he could perform, He never ceased to amuse us with his cleverness and mischievous sense of humor. Our "Spencie" loved to play, retrieve Frisbees and swim. He loved and befriended anyone and everyone he met.

My husband and I had many friends in the Houston area, largely due to our affiliation with St. John's Retreat Center and Wildlife Sanctuary, located approximately 50 miles north of Houston in Montgomery, Texas. We purchased land to be near the Spiritual Center in 1987 and put a mobile home on our property. While we were shopping for a mobile home in 1993 and driving to and from dealerships, we discovered a Dachshund/Catahoula mix darting between cars in the middle of a very heavily-trafficked five-lane highway near Houston. She was extremely close to being hit by a car or a truck a number of times. I couldn't bear to watch her weave in and out of traffic. I closed my eyes and prayed that she make it to the other side of the highway and find her way to a safe and loving home.

Somehow, she did manage to make it safely across the highway and landed in the parking lot of a fast-food restaurant between the rubbish bins. She was hot, exhausted, filthy and smelly, and obviously dehydrated and hungry. We parked our car and got close to her. She was very friendly. Of course, she had no collar or identification tag, but it was obvious that she had not been abused, as she was not the slightest bit afraid of Norman, me, or anyone else, for that matter. She had also been spayed. It was fairly obvious to us that she was a dog who had somehow escaped from her home or backyard. It was a July afternoon and the heat and humidity were unbearable. We gave her some water and lifted her into the back seat of our rental car. We stopped at a grocery store and bought her a collar, leash, kibble, doggie shampoo and some treats and a food and water bowl. We stopped at a mobile home dealership nearby whose sales manager allowed us to hose down and shampoo the dog. We then took her to a vet in a mini-mall where she was examined and vaccinated. Clean and refreshed, the dog was happy to get back in our air-conditioned car. We stopped at a restaurant and bought her some hamburgers without buns or condiments. She gobbled them down. We then smuggled the 15-pound Dachshund mix into our hotel – and later learned that this hotel actually permitted dogs.

She was a welcome "guest" at the hotel, and we could walk her freely through the lobby and on the hotel's grounds. We named the dog **Sophie**, and spent the rest of our vacation in Montgomery with our brand new baby. We guessed her age to be about two years old. She was the sweetest, friendliest, and most well behaved dog I have ever known. We took her everywhere with us – and everyone we met (including the hotel staff) fell in love with this little "angel." She was truly a canine ambassador, for she adored every living creature, and children in particular. She was like a magnet – people were drawn to her and just seemed to fall in love with her. Although we could legally have only three dogs at our home in Los Angeles, there was no doubt that we would adopt this beautiful little girl and welcome her into our home and lives.

When we arrived in LA, she was introduced to her canine siblings and got along beautifully with Caesar, Spencer and Katie. These four dogs were my children and became members of my nuclear family. Unfortunately, we had lost our dear little Yorkie, Reggie, before adopting Spencer. Reggie had been our last link with our life in New York, and had been through much with us. We grieved his loss. He had enjoyed a long and happy life and died of old age.

Katie, Caesar, Spencer and Sophie took turns coming to work with me and went on rides and vacations with Norman and me. They accompanied us on errands, worked and played with us. There was nothing – no one – whose companionship we loved and enjoyed more dearly. They were an integral part of our family and our social lives. We spent our days off from work, weekends, evenings, vacations, and holidays with them – Thanksgiving, Christmas, Easter, Memorial Day, the Fourth of July, Halloween, etc. We enjoyed mealtimes, exercise, playtime, hiking in the mountains, and dodging waves at the beach. Overall, we shared many joyous and fulfilling years together with them in Los Angeles – moments, days, months and years for which we were profoundly grateful.

Such a good helper!

11

Chmeeze

Spencer

Kaitlyn

Sophie

My husband and I had been dreaming of moving away from the chaotic, stressful lifestyle and congestion of Los Angeles for a long time. We had many friends in Texas, and I had friends and colleagues both in Houston and Dallas. The Northridge Earthquake of January 1994 (we lived 2½ miles from its epicenter), was the straw that broke the proverbial camel's back. We were forced to move to a rental home while our house underwent repairs caused by the quake. The Red Cross, FEMA and the National Guard became new and unwelcome components of our daily life following the earthquake. Our home as well as our offices had been damaged; my office had not only been damaged, but had also been robbed by looters several times. My husband's office was flooded. The damage to our suburban shopping centers, restaurants, etc. totally transformed our lifestyle. After intensive soul-searching, discussion and reflection, and after extensively searching for homes in Houston, Dallas, and Charlottesville, Virginia, we decided to move to a northwest suburb of Dallas on a near 2½-acre beautiful treed parcel of land in "horse country" with a pond where we could have as many dogs as we wished. We could also have horses, cows, pigs, goats and just about any other animals we wanted to rescue.

It was not easy leaving friends, family and colleagues behind. We had lived in Los Angeles for sixteen years, but we also knew it was time for a fresh start – to begin anew. We moved to the Dallas area Memorial Day weekend of 1995. The suburb to which we relocated was full of hills, trees, ponds, creeks, rivers, horse farms, cattle ranches, and a lot of natural beauty. We adapted quickly and had profound appreciation of the serenity and beauty of the area. Our dogs were in "heaven" – our 2-acre fenced-in backyard incorporated a large pond full of catfish, perch, blue-gill, turtles, frogs, toads, blue herons, and egrets, among others. In addition, it had a wooded area and a pool with a waterfall. We were mesmerized by the magnificence, complexity, and intricacy of the natural world that surrounded us. Our dogs swam in the pond and chased the ducks and frogs. They were fascinated by the fish and made mostly futile efforts to catch them.

Our house near Dallas ... home sweet home!

Looking out over our dog-friendly back yard

CHLOE

A DOG'S LIFE

After we moved, I began to take horseback riding and dressage lessons. In the spring of 1996, we adopted our first Texas rescue dog, a beautiful medium-sized red dog with a white-tipped tail and four white-tipped paws who was a cross based on Beagle/Foxhound. She, her mother and siblings had been found at the side of a road by a member of a rescue organization. The rescue group was holding an off-site adoption event. The red dog was in a crate and had the saddest eyes I've ever seen. As soon as I looked into her beautiful sad eyes, I knew we had to adopt her. She had been named **Chloe**, and she became our fifth dog. She was seven months old when we brought her home and was gentle, loving and eager to please. Although she was initially a little intimidated by the other dogs, she quickly adapted. She went to obedience classes and had her own trainer. We fell in love with her as soon as we met her. She wanted nothing more than to love and be loved. We happily obliged.

From little to big in no time!

Within a few months of adopting Chloe, my husband found a medium-sized golden/white Chow/Golden Retriever mix dog in the middle of the road. He pulled over and managed to get her into his truck. Although we contacted neighbors and local veterinarians, no one knew anything about her. She was a sweet and affectionate dog whom we subsequently adopted and named **Tasha**. Tasha was very shy and gentle and became best friends with Chloe. We enjoyed watching the two "girlfriends" play together. Tasha, unfortunately, was the least accepted by all of our other dogs. She was "last on the totem pole" or hierarchy. In the dead of winter on a cold, icy January morning, the older, stronger and smarter dogs ganged up on her, wounding her badly. We took Tasha to our vet, and for awhile it looked as though she would make it. Unfortunately, there were complications associated with the injuries, and after several days of acute suffering, our vet called to let us know that she had died. We were heartbroken.

"Very interesting..."

In July of 1998, our beloved Caesar was diagnosed with terminal osteosarcoma (bone cancer) and was given six months to live. I cannot describe how devastated my husband and I were at this prognosis of our baby. He seemed so healthy and vibrant; it was impossible to believe that he was dying. It took us quite some time to grasp that our baby would not be with us for much longer. We researched osteosarcoma on the internet and in countless books and articles. We contacted animal experts and veterinary oncologists and took Caesar to numerous veterinary specialists, holistic and homeopathic vets, pet psychics, an occupational therapist with whom Caesar had regularly scheduled appointments, a traditional acupuncturist, and a laser acupuncturist, among others. We prayed; we enlisted the aid of massage therapists and a Reiki healer – in short, we did everything in our power to prolong Caesar's life and quality of life. Nothing could – or would – prevent the inevitable. We provided Caesar with in-house, around-the-clock hospice care and gave him the highest quality of life we were capable of providing. We mourned his suffering and his loss long before his actual death.

During the period preceding Caesar's death, I attempted to prepare for the inevitable void in my life, but preparation simply wasn't possible. I took Caesar with me everywhere, and cried constantly because I knew that in only a short while he would no longer be with me. I adored this special, vulnerable boy who had come so far. My world revolved around Caesar – his veterinary appointments, his prescriptions, his treatments and spending as much quality time with him as I could while I could. I cried uncontrollably in anticipation of the loss that was soon to be. I never ignored my other wonderful dogs, but there is no doubt that Caesar was the recipient of the greatest amount of care, affection and attention.

In the fall of 1998, knowing full well that Caesar's death was imminent and that we could not bear life without an Alaskan Malamute, we decided to adopt a rescue Mal from the Alaskan Malamute Assistance League. We could have purchased a dog from many breeders, but we chose to save the life of one in need. We wanted a female, as we did not want Caesar to be jealous of or threatened or injured by a younger, stronger male. It was our hope that a new female Mal would carry on and serve as Caesar's liaison and legacy.

Chmeeze loved his duckies

We contacted the directors of the Texas Alaskan Malamute Rescue located in Bellville and were referred by them to their North Texas division which was run by one of the loveliest human beings I have ever known and who was, subsequently, to become one of my closest and dearest friends ever. Her name was **Betty Christenson**, and, although she would never even remotely think of herself as a saint or heroine, she was as close to being one as any human being I have known. She was one of the kindest, most thoughtful, considerate, generous, compassionate and selfless people I've ever met. She exemplified patience and

Chris and Betty, our Rescue mentor

Texas Alaskan Malamute Rescue Association

Dedicated to the welfare of Alaskan Malamutes.

humility as well as self-sacrifice. She adored all animal and devoted her "retirement" years to rescuing animal (and people) in need. She and her husband, **Chris**, ha anywhere from 15-20 "rescue" Malamutes (as well a some mixed breeds) up for adoption on their smal property at any given time. As do so many wonderfu people involved in Rescue, they did everything: caring fostering; transporting needy animals to a vet or boarding facility; visiting shelters to ID or evaluate them, working at fundraising events; donating food, time, money supplies; working on the Rescue websites; responding to inquiries about lost, found, injured, or shelter dogs in need of rescue and ultimately finding "forever" home for these animals. Betty and Chris transported animal throughout the state and Southwest, tended to thes animals, and tirelessly worked to educate the public abou the Alaskan Malamute breed, the importance o vaccinating, spaying/neutering and the importance o adopting versus purchasing an animal – especially wher there are so many animals in need.

When I spoke with Betty for the first time, I explained ou desire to adopt a "rescue" Malamute. I explained Caesar's condition and our need to have a Malamute in ou household, that he was old and frail and irreplaceable. We loved Caesar beyond measure. As per the Rescue group requirements, Betty, representing the Rescue group, came to our home to meet us and determine if we and our home were "suitable" for the adoption of a Malamute. We had already filled out an application to ascertain if ou personalities, habits and our lifestyle, as well as we wer

were appropriate, acceptable, and "worthy" of being awarded the privilege of becoming a guardian of one of their prospective adoptees. The process was quite similar to that of adopting a human child.

We learned so much from Betty and the Texas Alaskan Malamute Rescue Association. We learned how deeply these people loved and cared for the breed, and for each and every single dog they rescued – every dog whose life they saved. The members of the rescue organization went to great lengths to save any animal they could. They provided a foster home (a temporary home) for an animal in need, along with vaccinations, spaying or neutering, health care, and teaching these animals obedience and socialization skills. Above all, they provided a safe haven and hope for the future of placing these animals with people that loved and appreciated and respected them.

Betty was gentle, tough and wise. She knew how deeply we "needed" and wanted another Malamute in our lives as Caesar was living out his final days. There were no suitable Mals available at that time that would fulfill our needs as well as the needs of one of their adoptee dogs. We were very depressed. We knew Caesar did not have long to live, and we definitely wanted him to spend time with and "get to know" the dog that we would adopt who would "take over" when our Caesar was gone.

We received a phone call one afternoon from Betty saying that there was an Alaskan Malamute/wolf mix that was going to be euthanized in a southeastern suburb of Dallas. She had been a stray that managed to elude capture for more than a month and had been roaming around the community. She was wily, clever, and agile and seemed to love children as she was seen around various elementary and high schools in the area. She was gentle and never hurt anyone – yet Animal Control finally captured this cagey girl, having shot her with a dart gun, which almost paralyzed her. She was placed in a shelter and declared "unadoptable." She was temporarily housed in a small barbed wire cage until her scheduled euthanasia. Betty called us about this dog, and we adopted her, sight unseen. I somehow knew that she was meant to belong with us.

KIANNA
FAIRWEATHER

Sedonia Kennicoot Fairweather

"DONY"

Using her powerful charm and special "magic," Betty managed to persuade the personnel at the Animal Shelter to allow us to adopt the dog we named **Kianna Fairweather.** She and Chris went to pick her up and bring her over to our home. We knew she had advanced heartworm and had had surgery to repair the dart injury. She had also been a stray on the streets for over a month. Betty warned us that Kianna was emaciated and extremely frail. No matter how much negative information we received about her, we *knew* she was meant to be with us. I bought her a turquoise collar and leash and color-coordinated accessories. When Betty and Chris arrived at our home with Kianna, my heart leaped to my throat. My instincts had been correct – Kianna was the most beautiful dog I had ever seen – noble, majestic, regal and incredibly intelligent and intuitive.

We adopted Kianna on November 21, 1998. She was vaccinated and received extensive treatment for her heartworm disease. However, this did not prevent her from eating our entire Thanksgiving ham along with turkey and all of the holiday goodies that she ingeniously discovered by "counter surfing" through our kitchen. She was gaining weight; however, we attributed that to a healthy diet. We were wrong. Early in December, we discovered she was pregnant with a litter of eight or nine puppies. She gave birth to them on the evening of Christmas Day. Tragically, eight of the nine puppies died. We took them one by one to the emergency clinic throughout the night. The only one that managed to survive was the most precious puppy in the world to us– a beautiful white dog we named **Sedonia Kennicoot Fairweather (Dony)**.

Dony was very tiny and didn't open her eyes until two weeks after her birth. After losing all the other puppies, we were deeply concerned that all the vaccinations, surgery and heartworm treatments that Kianna had received would cause her puppy to be deaf, blind, afflicted or disabled in some way. Regardless of any potential health problems, we were dedicated and determined to give her the best possible life we could. Miraculously, our Christmas baby turned out to be perfect and beautiful like her mother.

Dony,
all grown up

Caesar died on December 28, 1998 – one of the saddest days of my life. As I had hoped, he died peacefully, surrounded by his loved ones in our den where we had spent so many joyful times together. We had a prayer service for him and played our favorite classical and spiritual music throughout the service. Our vet came to our home to administer euthanasia. We hugged and kissed our baby boy good-bye, thanking God and him for the privilege of being a part of our lives for so long and realizing that an era of our lives had come to an end and that there would never, ever be another like Caesar. We were devastated and in shock, we could not fathom life without our boy…

Caesar's death was a turning point for me. Although I had lost many loved ones and experienced many losses in my life, I had never grieved to the extent that I did for Caesar. I cried uncontrollably, lost my temper frequently, couldn't eat, couldn't sleep, couldn't focus or concentrate, was depressed and in despair. Even well-intentioned friends and family members advised me that "he was just a dog" and that I had "other dogs." I isolated myself from friends and family. I had virtually no interest in anyone or anything. No one seemed to grasp how deeply I had loved Caesar and how much he had meant to me. He had transformed my life – he was so fragile and delicate. I was his caregiver, the one he trusted above all. His eyes had always shone with gratitude and love. The pain I felt was agonizing. I missed him constantly

– his physical presence, his beauty, innocence, vulnerability, and the purity of his spirit. There was a huge void in my life, and life itself seemed meaningless and purposeless without him, I wanted desperately to be with him wherever he was.

Both Katie (as Caesar's lifelong companion) and Kianna seemed to understand my deep sadness. They would lie down with me as Caesar had, and surprisingly, Kianna exhibited certain habits, traits and mannerisms that only Caesar had had. It was as though Caesar had indeed communicated with Kianna and shared his understanding of my needs and me with her. It was obvious that Katie dearly missed her beloved friend. They had been inseparable for so many years. She had lain beside him throughout their lives together and throughout his illness. Katie had been Caesar's best friend and mine as well. She was receptive to Kianna's attempts to befriend her. But she had known Caesar better than anyone and been responsible for Caesar's becoming a part of our famiy, and there is no question in my mind that she was mourning his loss.

At this time, I searched for answers regarding the meaning of life and death – what purpose Caesar's life had served and why he had died – and read extensively about grief and loss and specifically, the loss of a pet. It seemed that there were very limited resources available to someone who had lost a beloved pet, and I was inspired both to receive training and certification as a Grief Recovery Specialist so that I could help others who were experiencing grief over the loss of a beloved pet. After Caesar's death, I wrote a book for children and their families called *When Your Pet Dies*, and I created and established the Pet Grief Counseling Program in association with the SPCA of Texas.

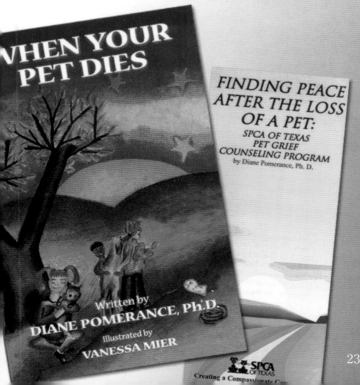

JASMINE

As a volunteer for the SPCA, of course I came into contact with many of the animals housed there who were hoping to be adopted. One of the first dogs I saw was an eight-year-old yellow Labrador Retriever named **Jasmine**. She was middle-aged and overweight and one of the saddest looking dogs I think I've ever seen. She had been turned into the SPCA because she was very heavily heartworm positive. The chances of her getting adopted were very slim. I decided to adopt her. I brought her home, and as soon as she saw our pond, she leaped into it and began to swim. She was exhilarated to be in the water. Unfortunately, her health deteriorated and she grew weaker and weaker. She was hospitalized and put on IV fluids, but it was obvious that she was dying. We brought her home from the veterinary hospital. As soon as she set foot in our back yard, she slowly and unsteadily made her way to the pond. We knew she wanted to swim, but she was far too ill and so she simply lay down. She died on the shore of the pond that she loved so much…We had come to love her dearly in the short time we knew her – we would never forget her innate dignity and gentle spirit.

Approximately three months after Caesar's death, we adopted another dog, a German Shepherd who had been terribly abused and abandoned, chained to a tree in his backyard after his "family" moved out. This dog had been taunted, left without food and water, and been damaged by both physical and verbal abuse. No one wanted him – there was nowhere for him to go. Some neighbors of his family managed to find us and begged us to adopt this dog that had suffered so greatly. There was a rainbow in the late afternoon sky the day that **Bentley** came to live with us. It seemed to signify hope for this heretofore "hopeless" boy. Bentley was keenly intelligent and well-mannered. He was "in heaven" living with us and his canine siblings – he swam, ran and played. I fell in love with this gentle, pitiful boy immediately.

Not long after we adopted Bentley, we learned of two Alaskan Malamute brothers who had arrived at the SPCA of Texas and were thought to be wolves. They were seven months old and were to be euthanized. My husband and I went to provide a breed identification for TAMR – they were indeed Malamutes

BENTLEY

KOBUCK

NENANI

nd biological brothers (littermates). We brought them home, and they became our ninth and tenth dogs. We alled the larger "wooly" brother **Kobuck**, and the smaller one that closely resembled a wolf, **Nenani**.

TOBIAS

We became very actively involved with Alaskan Malamute Rescue and helped Betty to screen potential homes and foster families, to help care and find homes for her Rescue dogs, and to assist her in any way we could. One Sunday afternoon at Betty's home, she showed us a photo album of the dogs she had rescued and those who were available for adoption. One of the dogs was Betty's favorite and especially gorgeous – his name was **Toby** and he had been treated for advanced heartworm disease and almost died. He had been shot many times with buckshot, had terrible arthritis, a fractured hip and other health issues. Betty and Chris pulled him through his heartworm and were looking for a home for him. The man who was fostering him brought him over to meet us that afternoon. He was a small Mal with a twinkle in his large brown eyes. He reminded us of Caesar, and we immediately fell in love with him. We re-named him **Tobias** and eventually referred to him as "Sir Tobes" He and Sophie were best friends and our first Canine Good Citizens and certified Therapy Dogs. They visited patients in hospitals and assisted living centers and worked with special needs children and adults, performing small miracles as "animal assisted therapy" dogs.

mm... tasty ball!

25

HITCHCOCK

The next dog we adopted was a beautiful brown and cream six- to seven-month-old Siberian Husky named **Hitchcock.** He was at the SPCA and was a real "talker." All the volunteers loved him – he was very friendly and outgoing and amused and entertained everyone who walked by his kennel, hopping up and down and howling and "speaking" as if trying to let people know that there had been some mistake and that he certainly did not belong in this strange place with so many other frightened and miserable dogs. One of his ears stood up and the other flopped down. The SPCA volunteers adored him and encouraged me to adopt him, and adopt him I did! Hitchcock was very playful and intelligent, and he, too, became one of our Therapy dogs.

← Not THAT Hitchcock

unny, our "diving" dog, is the quintessential Labrador etriever – fearless, loyal, loving, friendly and captivating. ood-natured and possessed with a wild and wonderful ersonality, we adopted her at the age of six months from family that did not want her and was planning on "getting d of her" one way or another. This poor pup had no ackyard and lived in a travel kennel far too small for her. he had eye problems and underwent entropic eyelid urgery. Her head was badly scarred – obviously the vidence of having been beaten and trying to get out of er small prison. Today, Sunny runs and swims to her eart's content. She dives in our swimming pool and wims laps in our pond. She is never happier than when n the water or simply just wet!

SUNNY

One year after Caesar's death, Spencer was diagnosed with Degenerative Myleopathy, a neurological and muscular disorder similar to Multiple Sclerosis or ALS ("Lou Gehrig's Disease") in humans. It is a degenerative neuro-logical disease that is chronic and progressive. The symptoms include hindquarter weakness, rear limb ataxia, loss of balance, difficulty getting up or lying down, knuckling while walking, and hoarseness of bark. Spencer displayed all of these. He began to fall and walked very unsteadily. He was puzzled by his condition and seemed unable to comprehend why he was constantly falling down. We provided him with every possible kind of veterinary care possible, but he was estimated to be about 13 years old, and he grew weaker and weaker. It was almost unbearable to watch his degeneration and deterioration. He had been very strong and muscular – now he was losing weight and was very weak and frail. His mind was as sharp as ever, and he never whined or complained about his condition, Rather, he seemed to adhere to the philosophy of "Keep On Keeping On."

He was stoic and happy-go-lucky and heroic in our eyes we, who administered his medications and took him t constant visits with our vet and specialists. We could no help but be impressed by how brave and trusting he wa He trusted us with every fiber of his being, and we woul have done everything in our power to minimize or eradicat his pain and disabilities. No longer able to walk, he was als incontinent. After some time, he was no longer willing o able to eat and was vomiting blood. When it was apparen that he was no longer enjoying any quality of life, we ha him euthanized in the comfort of our home with his lovin friends and family by his side.

At the time our Spencer was dying, we rescued a Alaskan Malamute/Siberian Husky mix that ha been picked up off of a country road and taken t Animal Control. We named him **Innoko**. He wa full of ticks and fleas and potentially dangerous t our Spencer's weakened immune system, and so Betty agreed to keep Innoko until we could safel bring him to live in our home. Innoko was very sh but his eyes danced merrily and he was ver mischievous and inquisitive. He was quiet an reserved, but he was a playful boy who managed t create a game out of any situation. Betty kep Innoko until she died of esophageal cancer in Marcl 2004. He brought her great joy, love, and laughte throughout the years they spent together.

"Aunt Betty, get me outa here!"

INNOKO

One year after Spencer's death, our magnificent Katie died. She was a member of our family for nearly 14 years. She had terrible hip dysplasia, lost sight in her left eye, and became immobile and incontinent. We literally carried her from room to room and in and out of the car. Katie was an extension of me – she was highly telepathic and seemed to understand me more than anyone else. I loved being with her – her presence was always comforting and calming. The thought of losing her was unbearable. As she became increasingly weak and frail, I slept with her on the floor in our den. I couldn't imagine life without my Katie. I loved her more than anyone. She was the best dog I have ever had. After giving her the finest medical and hospice care we could provide, she died peacefully in her sleep on June 2, 2003.

Our rescue angel

BOJANGLES

We adopted another of Betty's dogs after she died, an old and frail Siberian Husky mix named **Bojangles**. Bojangles was a whiner and a screecher, but he was also very intelligent, crafty and manipulative. He was Innoko's best friend and playmate. He had severe arthritis and hip dysplasia and could hardly walk, but he, too, made the best of his circumstances and refused to give up. His spirit was great, and his willpower and determination strong. He was an inspiration to us, and despite his physical ailments and problems, he was grateful to be alive and to be living with us.

After having had a German Shepherd, I decided that I could not be without one, so in 2004 we adopted a German Shepherd we named **Emily.** Although Emily looked like a smaller version of Katie, she was nothing like her. We purchased Emily from a reputable breeder, but Emily was the runt of the litter. She "talks" all the time and has boundless energy. She somehow manages to annoy or provoke all the other dogs as well as my husband and me. She loves stirring up trouble and revels in the attention caused by her bad behavior. We call her our "prom queen" and "social director" as she is always attempting to choreograph activities and engage the others in play.

EMILY

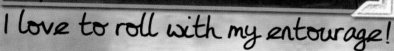

I love to roll with my entourage!

SHADOW

We adopted **Shadow**, an exquisite black and white nine-year-old Siberian Husky with slightly crossed ice blue eyes who had been surrendered to the SPCA because of the sudden development of a family member's "allergies." Shadow was extremely clever, wily and talkative. He was also very loyal and friendly. He was obviously heartbroken and terrified to be separated from his family of nine years and abandoned to an animal shelter. He howled constantly as though he were in excruciating pain. His mournful howling could be heard throughout the shelter. His chances of finding a home were very limited because of his age and because he had an advanced case of heartworm disease as well as a heart murmur. Shadow calmed down the moment I laid eyes upon him. He trusted me, and I loved him. I took Shadow home with me. He was a remarkable dog with a great

...in the shadows...

spirit. He was a wonderful therapy dog who visited the sick and elderly and disabled. He loved being admired, and he performed many "tricks" that entertained his "patients" as well as our friends and family members. He also assisted me at grief groups at the SPCA for years. As he grew older and sicker, he became more cantankerous and curmudgeonly, but we understood each other, and he remained one of the most beautiful, loyal and loving dogs I have ever known.

CINDERS

Cinders was also an SPCA dog who was owner surrendered at nine year[s] old. She was a beautiful purebred Siberian Husky with penetrating blu[e] eyes and very dainty features. She was well-behaved and sweet. We couldn['t] imagine why someone would give up a dog as lovely and intelligent a[s] Cinders was until we learned that she had cancer – mast cell tumors ove[r] almost her entire body. Rather than give her loving care and medica[l] attention she deserved, her owners had "given" her to the SPCA to "dispose[s]" of her. We had Cinders for only five month[s] before we had to have her put to slee[p]. During those five months, she enjoyed [a] wonderful life with her boyfriend Shado[w] and with her adoptive family with whom sh[e] celebrated Thanksgiving, Christmas, Ne[w] Year's and Valentine's Day, and from whom she received a great amount of love, affectio[n] and attention.

LUMBERJACK

After hearing of eleven-year-old **Lumberjack's** sad history, particularly the period following the bitter divorce of his human parents, we decided to have Betty bring him to our home on Thanksgiving day to spend the afternoon with him and to determine if he would get along with our other dogs. From the time we met, Betty and I always spent Thanksgiving, Christmas, Easter, Mother's Day and our birthdays together. Lumberjack was a very large and wooly Malamute who loved everyone and every being. He got along well with our dogs, and we ended up adopting him that day. Lumberjack was so grateful to have a loving home, and he expressed some of his gratitude in a unique way. He literally "sang" whenever he heard someone else singing. Although he could barely walk or see, he was a happy boy who loved to play and go for rides in the car. His previous owners left him outside in their yard night and day regardless of the season or weather. Lumberjack loved his new climate-controlled environment. He was full of love and joy. He loved to make us laugh!

MAXIMUS

Another "victim" of a bitter divorce and custody battle was our beloved Anatolian Shepherd, **Maximus**. I found out about his desperate situation from my friend and fellow member of my Visiting Therapy Dogs group, who for privacy's sake we'll call "Miranda." Miranda's father had taken the beloved family dog and "couch potato," Max, and kept him locked in a gardening shed (neglected and abused) for four years after telling his daughter that Max had died. Her father's ex-girlfriend told Miranda that Max was indeed still alive but living under horrific conditions with no food, little water and no human interaction. Miranda located Max and was reunited with her once healthy, robust dog whom she had always adored, only to find that he was emaciated, had tumors all over his large body and was in need of extensive medical care. As Miranda was a college student living in an apartment that forbade dogs, we adopted him. He was 10½ years old. He lived with us for three years, during which he became an outstanding Therapy Dog and great friend to everyone he met. Despite his age and infirmities, Max was the most good-natured and loving dog one could ever want. He never whined – he was always happy and ready to play with tennis or soccer balls. He loved playing with children and was very gentle. He was truly an "angel."

"Step on it, Dad!"

KHANTI

DIVA

Khanti is a beautiful gold and white Malamute with a life-threatening blood disease. We adopted her from a local shelter where we did a breed identification for Rescue. She is on a multitude of medications but is only four to five years old. She is very loving, affectionate, and strong-willed. She dutifully takes her medicine and treatments without complaint. It is sad that she does not run and play with the other dogs, but prefers to lie quietly and rest in her air-conditioned room.

We adopted ten-year old **Diva** from a local shelter – another owner surrender because she was simply too old and "demanding" to keep. I was providing breed identification for Malamute Rescue when I first met her. As I walked her down the shelter hallway, a mother and her three children asked if they could pet Diva. Diva gave the little ones big face kisses. One of the little girls asked her mother if she could bring Diva home with her. Her mother said, "We could never adopt a dog that old." It was with dread that I thought of Diva's future. She had been abandoned by her family at her old age. Sure, she was a stately, dignified old girl, but she was very young at heart, playful, spirited and talkative. I knew she would make a wonderful animal companion for whatever amount of time she had left. After taking her to our vet, who examined her and provided her with vaccinations, I couldn't wait to bring her home. I didn't care how old she was – I knew I could give her love and care for whatever weeks/ months/years she had left. She was a character with charisma and a powerful personality. She was very maternal and somewhat "bossy," especially when taking care of the younger dogs entrusted to her charge.

34

TALLON

Tallon was a 1½ year old Malamute that had come to live with us from Houston after Hurricane Katrina. Well-behaved for a puppy, he adjusted easily to his new home and siblings. Tallon is beautiful and very sweet, and is Innoko's playmate and best friend.

ANGEL

"Snow Angel"

Through Rescue, we learned of an elderly, ten-year-old female Malamute named **Angel** whose human father shot himself to death. Her father had been very ill and in a tremendous amount of pain. He had few friends and family members. Angel was his reason for getting up each morning. He adored her. She had been well-taken care of but then found herself homeless. We visited Angel at a boarding kennel – again to identify her as a Malamute – so that Rescue might find a foster home for her. We saw Angel – a "textbook" example of a purebred Malamute. We knew that we had to bring her home with us. Angel was very intelligent, wily and feisty. She and Diva took turns "mothering" the younger dogs and vying to be "top dog" – literally.

Mara came to live with us after she had been hit by a car on a busy street. She was paralyzed when we first received word of her, and several local veterinarians gave her a five percent chance of ever walking again. However, one of our friends, who is an animal chiropractor, worked with Mara. Through her efforts and Mara's determination and will, Mara not only walked again but also ran. Her gait is irregular and awkward, but she is able to play and swim and chase her brothers and sisters.

HIGGINS HIGGINS

Higgins, a two- or three-year-old Malamute/Lab mix, was in the euthanasia room in southern Texas waiting to be put down. Rescue intervened and we agreed to take him in. He is beautiful, gentle, and highly intelligent. Higgins is his Dad's "favorite" dog (don't tell the others!) because his personality is most like Caesar's. We adopted Higgins in June 2007.

CLARISSA CLARI

We adopted Clarissa, a purebred Anatolian Shepherd, in 2007 in honor of our dear Max. She was destined to be euthanized – she was flea- and tick-infested and so very depressed. She was painfully thin – half of one of her ears had been ripped off, and she was very shy. Not for long. Today, she is a vision of Anatolian joy and beauty with a droll wit and sense of humor. We laughingly refer to her as our "guard dog," as she is the size of a Mastiff and looks and barks intimidatingly. She is, however, "all bark and no bite."

36

GINS   HIGGINS

CLARISSA   CLARISSA

Our beloved Sophie died on November 12, 2005. Once again, our hearts were broken. Sophie had Cushing's Disease, a severe heart murmur, several strokes and was almost fourteen years old. She was truly an angel and a gift from God. She was the last member of our "nuclear" family, which had consisted of Katie, Caesar, and Spencer, and Sophie.

"The Dachshunds" are a family unto themselves as well as members of our extended canine family. They know that they are "The Dachshunds" and come and kiss and cuddle with us whenever they hear the phrase spoken. **Phoebe** came into our lives in January 2006. She had been a puppy mill dog and had been at the SPCA of Houston until she was taken into a loving foster home by the Dachshund Rescue of Houston Organization, one of the finest rescue organizations I have ever known. I drove down to Houston on Martin Luther King Jr. Day to pick her up from her foster "Mom." Phoebe reminds me so much of Sophie. She is gentle, loving, devoted to Norman and me, and very maternal. She is also very sensitive, solicitous, and concerned with the welfare and wellbeing of her canine siblings.

PHOEBE

hs·hund: \'däks-hunt, -hund; 'däk-sənt; ecially British 'dak-sənd\ (noun) erman, from *Dachs* badger + *Hund* dog] : ny of a breed of looooooooooooong-bodied, hort-legged dogs of German origin ...

Luddy entered our lives – he had been hit by a car and had a broken leg, was heartworm positive and emaciated, and had other health issues. Because of all of his health problems, he was not regarded as adoptable. Nonetheless, he found a home with us. He has such a powerful personality and presence and is adored and pampered by the other dogs and his parents. He views himself as the small but venerable and powerful ruler of the household.

LUDLOW

Ve adopted **Coco**, another puppy mill Dachshund – a irl who apparently was a breeding female who was bred nany, many times, judging from the scars on her bdomen and chest. She is too large to appeal to those ho want the smaller breeds. She is gentle, affectionate nd wise. She is very loving, beautiful and smart. She is ery well-mannered, and we adore her.

COCO

Two Socks is a very, very special young Malamute who had been terribly abused by his "family" who did not feed him or provide him with water. They kept him tethered to their mobile home and outside all year round. They did not interact with him at all, and, when they moved away, they left him behind. He became a stray – virtually feral. This helpless dog was the saddest, loneliest, and most pitiful dog I have personally known. He was absolutely terrified of people – of literally, everyone. He was malnourished, terribly dehydrated, had leptospirosis, Lyme disease, and his kidneys were failing. A member of Rescue called him a "project dog," meaning it would require enormous patience and effort to rehabilitate him. We adopted him in December 2007. I managed to gain his trust, and over a period of one year, he blossomed into a loving, grateful, beautiful boy who sleeps with us, plays with his siblings and us, goes for walks and rides in the car. He is still shy, but loves having his picture taken. He never seems to stop "smiling."

In October 2008, we saved the lives of three Malamutes – a mother and two of her puppies. We put the word out in hopes of getting these dogs adopted (they had been strays) and we boarded them at a nearby boarding facility. We adopted the daughter, **Shania**, who was very intelligent and beautiful. We brought her home, and by the second week she was with us, she displayed extremely dominant and aggressive behavior with our other dogs. She badly wounded Tallon, and she also physically injured the other dogs. We could not keep her, so we found a wonderful foster home for her through Rescue. She has subsequently found a wonderful "forever" home.

TWO SOCKS

LOL!

SHANIA

40

KALI

We ended up adopting Shania's brother, **Kali**, named for the Hindu god of mischief. His name could not be more appropriate. He is lovable, huggable, funny and mischievous, and he is gorgeous. Unlike his sister, he gets along well with everyone and is a wonderful ambassador for the Malamute breed. His gentle spirit and *joie de vivre* bring us great pleasure. We can't help but laugh at his antics and enjoy his friendly, good-natured personality. He loves to sing the Malamute "woo-woo" song and is very talkative!

Cassie is a Klee Kai – a "designer" breed, a miniature version of a combination of Siberian Husky/Alaskan Malamute/Schipperke and Eskimo dog. She was a stray who was picked up by Animal Control and believed to be a Malamute puppy. Wrong! She never grew larger, and we eventually discovered that she would be, in essence a miniature Mal/Husky mix. We adopted her in February 2009. She is Kali's age and his best friend. Cassie is beautiful, very refined and well-mannered. She and Kali are adorable and partners in crime together!

CASSIE

LUCADO

"ARF! I said turn it ARF!"

Lucado is a sly, impish, resourceful Malamute/German Shepherd mix, whose original owners gave her away to a friend of a friend who was ordered by her landlord to get rid of the dog. The dog was much too clever and and destructive and so, of course, we ended up providing her with a permanent home. Lucado was very weak and sick with heartworm disease but has recovered well from her third treatment. Despite her past illness, she is almost always involved in some kind of mischief or misadventure and creating chaos for Norman and me. She is an escape artist and a skilled and serious counter-surfer who snags and devours every kind of food imaginable, from cookies and crackers to avocados and Danish pastry from the kitchen counters, dining table, and kitchen table. Lucado makes me wish that I were a lot younger so that I could keep up with her antics. She is yet another "gift"(?) from God.

ELLIE

FRITZ

The most recent additions to our family are the Dachshund/MinPin mixes: one named **Fritz Henry,** who is black and tan, and **Eleanor Cricket,** who is dappled gray, tan and black. They are from the same litter and are about the same size, though Ellie's legs are longer. They are pure love. They adore and are completely devoted to each other. Phoebe, Coco and Luddy are now the proud "parents" of these new Dachshund/MinPin babies. They guard, supervise, discipline and socialize them. What a delight and joy it is to watch them all play and interact. Even at nine months old, the babies are so clever, resourceful and full of love, life and curiosity. They make me laugh and feel young again!

Always together, coming & going!

With "Mommy" Phoebe

43

Although our dogs have brought us unimaginable joy and fulfillment, it would be remiss and irresponsible of me not to mention the profound commitment, obligations and responsibilities as well as the enormous amount of work and effort (not to mention time and money!) required of my husband and me associated with the care and well-being of these animals. Our daily lives essentially revolve around their physical, social and emotional needs. Our schedules and both our professional and social lives are dictated in large part by the needs of our canine kids.

Our canine kids require gentle loving care, attention, patience and interaction; they are social, intelligent beings that thrive on companionship and respect. They require a healthy diet and plenty of fresh water. They need to be supervised and disciplined. They require exercise and plenty of playtime. Depending upon their age and health status, they may require a special diet and/or a rigorous regimen of medications and dietary supplements. They require shots and vaccinations and veterinary treatment on a regular basis. They should be bathed and groomed routinely. They need to be obedience-trained and socialized so that they are comfortable with and friendly toward fellow animals as well as their human companions. They need to learn to adjust to and behave well around other animals and humans.

If and when we are obliged to leave them for any reason, we make provisions for their care and wellbeing. If we are away for only a short while, we have a dogsitter come and play with them, feed them, and provide fresh water for them. If we are away longer than a few days, we make certain that our vet is notified and that the dogs are provided with live-in, in-house caregivers who are experienced, compassionate, and well-versed with our dogs' personalities, needs and daily routine. As always, we make certain that we have back-up vet techs, vets on notice, and friends who check up on our dogs and make sure our husband-and-wife dog-sitters are taking care of our canine kids. We supply our caregivers with a long and detailed list of instructions regarding when each group of dogs eats, is exercised, etc.

All 21 of our dogs are fed twice daily – in the morning and in the evening. Many are on special diets and medications, depending upon their age and physical condition. Therefore, feeding them is far more complicated than merely scooping some kibble into their bowls. The dogs are fed in six separate groups to prevent fighting or food-aggressive behavior. Food preparation and service can take up to two hours. Each group is let out in our back yard and exercised in the morning upon awakening and fed, then let out again after they have eaten. The groups are rotated throughout the day and into the night. Regardless of the season or weather, my husband or I walk and play with them, so that we are outside during rain and snow, sun and hail, blizzard and heat wave.

In between feeding and exercising the dogs, I do my best to get work done (writing, checking and returning emails, corresponding with those in need of advice about their pets and pet loss, providing telephone or one-on-one grief counseling, and doing radio or newspaper/magazine interviews). Each day presents me with a brand new set of problems or challenges, ranging from personal and family health issues to professional obligations, and relationship challenges. The dogs bring their own range of challenges. Is one of the dogs sick or lethargic? Do I wake up to discover diarrhea, vomit, or blood in any of the dogs' rooms? Are thunderstorms terrifying Kobuck, Khanti or Dony? How quickly can I give them acepromazine (a sedative) to calm them down? Are my dogs going to fight? Injure themselves?

A DAY IN MY LIFE by Diane

*Let me preface this section with the acknowledgment that there is absolutely no "typical" day in my life. I've done my best to convey an idea as to what a day or two are like. Here we go:

5:30 a.m. That darn alarm clock goes off. We hit the snooze button.

6:30 a.m. The darn alarm goes off again. This time I heed it and roll over, huddling under the covers. Norm gets up and heads to the kitchen to make some coffee and let each of the dog groups out in succession. In his pajamas and boots, he walks with those who need supervision (like our puppies). Each group of dogs barks in turn, so I couldn't possibly continue to sleep.

7:30 a.m. All the dogs are back inside.

7:30 a.m. Radio station calls me for an interview regarding seasonal pet care tips. Fortunately, this I can do without makeup.

7:30-7:45 a.m. Norm showers and dresses for work. He leaves by 7:45 - 7:50.

7:45-8:00 a.m. I force myself to get out of bed and check my emails and/or phone messages. I play with the dogs, get dressed; ready for my trek with each group of dogs. The bedroom group goes out first.

8:30- 10:00/10:30 a.m. Exercise each of the rest of 6 dog groups - 20 minutes each.

10:30 a.m. Prepare dog breakfast - puppy kibble, middle-aged kibble, senior kibble, small dog kibble, special needs kidney kibble, plus meds, supplements, etc. Throw in some food pellets for the turtles in our kitchen aquarium. The phone rings, and while I am engrossed in my call, Mara empties the kitchen garbage can. I pick up the trash and take it out. Replace garbage bag. Mop up floor. Tallon vomits in utility room. Mop up floor again.

11:00 a.m. Feed each group separately. Let them out in order they have eaten. Go out with Ellie and Fritz, Tallon, Kali, Lucado and Innoko. Go out with Hitchcock and walk him. Pick up poop in backyard with pooper-scooper.

    After each group eats, they go out again, I rinse out their bowls. I let them out, then follow up on emails, voice mail messages, and counseling.

1:00 p.m. Work on article for Internet magazine. Stop to clean up the toilet paper confetti shredded all over my bedroom by Phoebe and Emily.

(continued)

Chow time
chez Pomerance

45

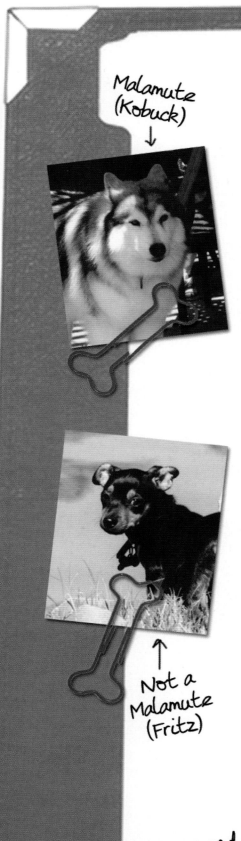

Malamute
(Kobuck)
↓

↑
Not a
Malamute
(Fritz)

2:00 p.m. Magazine interview regarding whether to purchase or adopt a pet.

3:00 p.m. Receive email regarding need for someone to breed-identify three Malamutes in a shelter in a nearby suburb. I respond and comply.

4:00 p.m. Arrive at Shelter and identify the dogs as Mals. They are believed to be a 2-year-old Mal mother and two of her pups, one male and one female, approximately a year old. I make arrangements for them to receive their vaccinations and to be spayed and neutered. So that they are not euthanized, my friend Lou and I arrange to board them at our favorite boarding facility in Argyle, Texas.

5:30 – 6:00 p.m. Arrive home. Check phone calls and emails. Begin preparation for making dogs' dinner. Process is similar to breakfast. They usually get roast chicken with rice, ground turkey, turkey breast, or lean ham, along with their kibble and meds.

6:30 – 9:00 p.m. Feed and walk six dog groups.

Prepare a bite of dinner for Norm and me, usually involving the ordering of "take-out" and setting up "to go" containers on table.

Return calls and provide pet grief phone counseling for several people who have contacted me via the SPCA or my website.

Bring last group of dogs in.

11:00 – 12:00 p.m. Shower, watch a few minutes of television, read an article about dogs who have thunderstorm phobias, set my dreaded alarm clock and attempt to fall asleep, wedged into the fetal position by three dachshunds, a German Shepherd and an Alaskan Malamute.

On second thought, maybe I'll try the sofa.

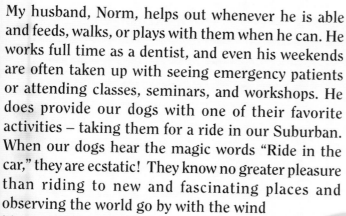

My husband, Norm, helps out whenever he is able and feeds, walks, or plays with them when he can. He works full time as a dentist, and even his weekends are often taken up with seeing emergency patients or attending classes, seminars, and workshops. He does provide our dogs with one of their favorite activities – taking them for a ride in our Suburban. When our dogs hear the magic words "Ride in the car," they are ecstatic! They know no greater pleasure than riding to new and fascinating places and observing the world go by with the wind blowing through their fur.

"Come on, Dad, let's go!"

Dr. Garry O'Neal setting up for vaccinations

Then, of course, our lives include countless visits to the vet for one reason another – as simple as a wound, cough, diarrhea or vomiting, or as serious a condition as heart disease, cancer, liver or kidney disease, leptospirosis, or diabetes. Our veterinarians, associated with the Argyle Vet Clinic in Argyle, Texas, have kindly and compassionately treated all of our dogs since we moved to Dallas. They have come to our home to examine and provide vaccines for 9-10 of my dogs at a time. They have also come, when necessary, to administer euthanasia.

OUR LIFESAVERS

LOU

As I work out of our home, I am surrounded by the dogs throughout the day as I work at the computer, talk on the phone, provide counseling, do radio interviews, visit with colleagues, entertain the never-ending stream of service people (electricians, plumbers, cleaning people, carpenters, air conditioning/heating, gardeners, etc.) who visit our home. Several people, including **Lou Olinger** and **Amber Kroeger**, assist me with my work and help me care for the dogs each weekday afternoon – all bona fide animal lovers and caregivers. Amber works Monday, Wednesday and Friday. Lou works Tuesday and Thursday afternoons. Up until Lou joined me two years ago, I did virtually all dog-related work/care by myself. It is only because of my co-workers who brainstorm with me and exercise the dogs in the afternoon, cleaning out their rooms, replenishing water, etc., that I have time to get any "real" work done. In the past, I had fewer dogs and would work primarily late in the night or early in the morning.

The dogs require careful and constant monitoring and attention. They are fearless, playful, courageous and mischievous. They love to chase squirrels and rabbits, ducks, and geese. They bark at our neighbor's dogs. Periodically, they will attack or fight with one another and injure themselves or each other. They require constant supervision and are our responsibility 24/7. We love them dearly, and in so many ways they are our "children." We provide them with whatever care and attention we deem advisable and appropriate.

AMBER

Adopting 21 dogs was never a part of our plan – that is, unless we were the owners and directors of an "official" animal sanctuary. But Life works in mysterious ways, and we have, for many reasons (many unbeknownst to us), been entrusted with the guardianship of these delightful animals that teach us so much about Life each and every day. Once we have made the decision to adopt them, they have become our responsibility. We are responsible for their health, welfare, and well-being – in essence, their very lives. They become members of our family, and we are not only their guardians but also their "parents."

Through the adoption of many older and special needs animals, we have learned, much about pain and suffering, about loss and grief. We have nursed so many through serious illnesses and diseases. Some have survived; others have not. We have provided hospice care more often than I care to remember. We have experienced fear, helplessness, and anguish as we have witnessed the pain and suffering of such innocent creatures. We have also witnessed the grace, stoicism and dignity of our beautiful animals as they suffer and die. We have done our best to alleviate their pain and suffering. There is such an intense and powerful emotional bond that develops between us and each dog we adopt. Each one is special – each is beautiful – each brings unique gifts and blessings. Each loss is heartbreaking and devastating. Loss never becomes easier; each loss is excruciatingly and indescribably painful.

Our 21 Current Canine Kids:
Emily, Phoebe, Clarissa
Cassie, Innoko, Hitchcock
Luddy, Higgins, Tallon
Kali, Dony, Nani
Mara, Khanti, Sunny
Fritz, Ellie, Two Socks
Lucado, Kobuck, Coco

49

As I write this book, I am reminded of the extraordinary experiences, opportunities, and blessings that have been mine in knowing and loving each of the remarkable animals that has been a part of my life. Despite the drudgery and stress of our daily lives together, we share so much joy, laughter, and excitement. Each dog evokes special moments and memories and a very special kind of love and beauty. As I reflect upon my life with them, I cannot feel anything other than profound gratitude for the privilege of sharing my life with them.

The joy of saving the life of or "rescuing" an animal is indescribable. We have been so blessed and privileged to share life with those who have suffered so deeply, and who not only survive, but blossom and flourish. From them, we have learned so many and profound lessons about love, life and death and derived such great peace, pleasure and fulfillment. I would not exchange these experiences for anything!

... in every season ...

Our dogs are our FAMILY!

51

Epilogue: Our Rescue Dogs and the Holidays

The holidays, Thanksgiving and Christmas, in particular, have always held deep meaning, richness of spirit, holiness, fun and joy for Norman and me. With the adoption of our special dogs throughout the years, the holidays have assumed an even greater significance and an opportunity to further appreciate and express our gratitude for the countless gifts and blessings that are ours.

Our dogs have served as a powerful link to the Divine Creative Force responsible for life and our planet, solar system, galaxy as well as to the world of Nature. As the seasons change, it has become ever more obvious that Beauty and Wonderment are a part of our daily lives, both inner and outer. We become touched and transformed as our animals respond to the poetry of the changing world around them. They embrace the crisp autumn air and welcome the return of the ducks and geese in their pond after their northern summer hiatus. With the approach of winter, their zest for life seems to increase and their playfulness intensifies. It becomes easier for them to spot the cardinals and blue herons, to chase squirrels and to revel in the crispness, crackle and special fragrance of fallen leaves. The first snowfall and icing become the background and object of enormous fun, anticipation, excitement, exhilaration and a variety of brand new games.

We share the joys of the seasons and the beauty and bounty of the holidays with our babies. We are so grateful for whatever time we have with them and are especially thankful for the joy and comfort and extra interaction we can share with them.

Thanksgiving is precisely that: a time for us to enjoy and give thanks for our loved ones – human and animal. It is a time to reflect upon our lives – the joys and sorrows – and to cozily embrace our family and friends.

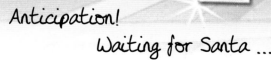

Anticipation!
Waiting for Santa ...

There is no forced gaiety or piety – only genuine appreciation and respect for our lives and the opportunity to share a feast composed of our favorite treats and spend quality time playing and simply being with those we love and with whom we can truly be ourselves – without pretense, agenda, protocol or façade.

Christmas reminds us of the birth of a Great and Holy One, and the gifts and knowledge associated with His life and teaching. We acknowledge the presence and presents each of our friends and family members has given us –spiritual growth and expanded awareness as well as the physical beauty and comfort each has provided.

We are so grateful to know each and every one of them – and to learn that all are purposeful and meaningful. On another level, we love the music, festivities, food, light, traditions, rituals and lovely ornaments and decorations associated with the holiday. Sometimes we will attend Christmas Eve Mass and bring our doggies in the car with us. As soon as the service is over, we head home and have a special Christmas Eve dinner and playtime. That evening and the following morning (Christmas Day), we derive special pleasure (I think we, more than the dogs actually do) as they open and play with their holiday gifts.

We truly enjoy and appreciate the special warmth and peacefulness of the time we spend together during this engaging and "magical" time of year. We enjoy sharing our beautiful canine kids and their antics with our friends, colleagues, and fellow animal lovers. We take a collective sigh of relief and rejoice that for at least a brief time, we can embrace life as children—with joy, cheer, goodwill, spontaneity—and fun!

Some of Our Favorite Quotations

Dony and Kianna

"Our task must be to free ourselves by widening our circle of compassion to embrace all living creatures and the whole of nature and its beauty."

— *Albert Einstein*

Bentley

"The worst sin toward our fellow creatures is not to hate them, but to be indifferent to them; that's the essence of inhumanity."

— *George Bernard Shaw*

"The greatness of a nation and its moral progress can be judged by the way its animals are treated."
— *Mohandas Gandhi*

Katie

"One touch of nature makes
the whole world kin."
— *William Shakespeare*

Dony and Spencer

"Spencer Bob"

"You may call God love, you may call God goodness.
But the best name for God is compassion."
— *Meister Eckhart*

"Compassion is the basis of morality."
— *Arnold Schopenhauer*

"It should not be believed that all beings exist for the sake of the existence of man. On the contrary, all the other beings too have been intended for their own sakes and not for the sake of something else."
— *Maimonides*

Clarissa

"If a man is not to stifle his human feelings, he must practice kindness towards animals, for he who is cruel to animals becomes hard also in his dealings with men. We can judge the heart of a man by his treatment of animals."

— *Immanuel Kant*

"Alone we can do so little . . .
together we can do so much."
— *Helen Keller*

Our Extended Family
Front Row: Lou Olinger (with Mara), Dr. Diane Pomerance, Donna Jones.
Center: Amber Kroeger, Cassie, Higgins, Dr. Norman Pomerance.
Back Row: Katrina Tiner, Dick Olinger.

About the Author

Diane Pomerance received her Ph.D. in Communications from the University of Michigan, Ann Arbor. She has been certified as a Grief Recovery Specialist by the internationally recognized Grief Recovery Institute. She was trained directly by the founder of the Institute, John W. James. Dr. Pomerance counsels those grieving from any loss; however, she has a special interest in helping those mourning the loss of a beloved companion animal. The loss of a pet can be devastating to adults as well as children.

Dr. Pomerance created, established and serves as director of the Pet Grief Counseling Program for the SPCA of Texas. In addition to serving as an active volunteer for the SPCA of Texas, she is a strong supporter of the Alaskan Malamute Assistance League, Texas Alaskan Malamute Rescue Association, and TvAMAL (Texas Volunteers for the Alaskan Malamute Assistance League) and Dachshund Rescue of Houston. She is frequently interviewed as a highly qualified "pet expert" on national television and radio programs and has been interviewed in many newspapers and magazines including *The Los Angeles Daily News, The Dallas Morning News, The Fort Worth Star-Telegram, Redbook, Quick & Simple, Woman's World, WomansDay.com,* and *Washington Times.* She has been an online expert for *Cat Fancy* Magazine and featured on www.WebMD, as well as a guest expert on such nationally syndicated TV programs as "Fox and Friends," "The Montel Williams Show," Hallmark Channel's "New Morning," "The Daily Buzz," "Your Health," and Fox News "Happening Now." She has also been a guest on the Dallas/Fort Worth network news affiliated stations and stations throughout the country.

She is the author of numerous articles and the highly acclaimed books, *When Your Pet Dies; Animal Companions: Your Friends, Teachers & Guides; Animal Companions: In Our Hearts, Our Lives, & Our World; Animal Elders: Caring About Our Aging Animal Companions; Finding Peace After the Loss of a Loved Animal Companion;* and *Pet Parenthood: Adopting the Right Animal Companion for You* and is the writer/performer of the books' accompanying audio CDs. She lives in North Texas with her husband and numerous canine "kids."